To Deidre Flaye without whose help this book would never have been written

Lottie Freeman who we all knew as 'Mum' and who left us June 29th 1992

THEYDON BOIS

– AND ALL THAT –

By Jack Farmer

Published by:

J.R. Farmer
Beech House,
65, Theydon Park Road,
Theydon Bois,
Essex CM16 7LR.

ISBN 0 9507367 8 3

Printed by:

Metloc Printers Ltd.,
Caxton House,
Old Station Road,
Loughton,
Essex IG10 4PE
Telephone: 081-502 0236

The ancient Theydon Bois Parish Church, known to be in existence in 1253 but believed to have been much older. This church was pulled down in 1844

John Robert Farmer, better known as Jack was born in Westgrove, Woodford, on October 2nd, 1911. Educated at Woodford Green and Loughton Schools, he began his career in the motor trade in 1927 at Wood and Krailing's Garage, and rose to become Managing Director.

Since retiring he has written four previous books; Theydon Bois As I Knew It In 1980; Epping Town Fire Brigade In 1983; Woodford As I Knew It In 1986; and the Great Eastern Railway As I Knew It In 1990.

The Author 'Et son chien'

The original Theydon Bois Village sign, produced and painted in 1950 by Bill Large, the well known commercial artist who lived in the village

The 'restored' village sign. Gone is the magnificent stag, replaced by this somewhat insipid example. Far more serious, is that the Forestry Crown so carefully copied by Bill Large, has been altered in shape, while the ancient cattle branding mark peculiar to Theydon Bois, has been left off altogether!

PREFACE

My previous book 'Theydon Bois as I knew it' was written about local people, and of events which took place during this Century. My decision to write was taken because it was necessary to correct the great many errors and omissions which appeared in a booklet published in 1977. To my great surprise and pleasure some 1600 copies have been sold, a number finding their way to the U.S.A., Canada, Australia and New Zealand.

This book is the story of how our Village might have evolved and developed from early times. Though it is fictitious, much is based on fact, what is more it gives me the opportunity of describing my own personal experiences of how the poor lived early in this Century. As I am able to trace my ancestry back in this part of Essex for almost 200 years, and because I am the youngest son of a youngest son, it means that I grew up surrounded by elderly relatives, who would constantly hark back to the middle of the last Century. Consequently much of what they talked about "rubbed off" on me so that I am in a rather unique position to write a tale such as this. Whichever way you look at it, I hope you will enjoy reading this story.

INTRODUCTION

It has always puzzled me why historians will never accept a simple derivation of the name of a place or district, but will go to endless trouble to produce some obscure theory. Thus we have "the Valley where the thatch grows", and the "Thegn on the Hill", supposedly of this area.

In 1966 we celebrated '1066 and all that', which was the 900th anniversary of the date William the Conqueror invaded these shores. The Domesday Book which he ordered to be made, divided this country into various Manors and Hundreds. To name these must have been fairly straightforward where there was a Town or Village already in existence, but huge tracts of land, such as the Great Waltham Forest, which at one time covered 60,000 acres, must have been given names by his surveyors. Certainly the similarity of some of these suggests it!

But even this truly monumental work, must be looked at in its proper perspective. One has to remember these islands were inhabited centuries before King William arrived, and changes in our ancient language took place when the Romans, Norsemen, Danes, and the Anglo Saxons invaded us in their turn.

Then the dialects in different parts of the Country were much more pronounced in those early days of sparse communications amounting almost to foreign languages in their own right! The ancient word Don for a hill, and peculiar to this part of Essex is an example, so that even today with everybody on the move, there are still peculiarities, and pockets where the old vernacular is used in Essex, I will relate two little stories to illustrate this.

The first concerns a lady looking for an address in Bobbingworth, only to find when eventually arriving at the Post Office, the word Bovinger over the door! How was she to know the place used two names?

The other is about the motorist who asked the way from a local, and was told he should take the road through Winnigal. It was some time before he found out the place was Willingale!

I have therefore written this story for your edification, and, I hope, enjoyment. Inevitably I have had to use my imagination to bridge some of the gaps, but I have included every scrap of authentic information I have acquired during my lifetime, which includes 65 years close connection with Theydon Bois. Because of the interest shown in 1066 and the Domesday Book, I am beginning my story at that time, and have chosen what I think is an appropriate title for it.

I cannot conclude this introduction without paying tribute to the late Rev. E.F.W. Ames, whose little book "Theydon Bois past and present" has been such a help to me in the early part of this work.

Jack Farmer - 1992

This superb photograph of St. Mary's Church by Percy Wilkins has never I think been equalled

THEYDON BOIS AND ALL THAT

It is the year 1066, and England has just been invaded by William of Normandy, though this momentous event has had little or no effect on this part of the Great Waltham Forest where we now live! An area covered mainly by Oak and Hornbeam trees, for the all-conquering Beech had not yet made its appearance. Growing faster and taller than the Oak, it was destined to smother the latter out of existence, or reduce it to a shadow of its normal size, for the Oak needs three things if it is to grow to its majestic maturity, light, space, and above all time! There was very little activity here; a traveller making his way through the forest, a woodman seeking suitable trees for the King's ships, or wood for building houses. Here the Hornbeam came into its own, for the wood is very hard and gets harder with age, so that it is almost impossible to saw, as I know from personal experience. This tree has another useful property, for after lopping, it puts out young shoots which in time will supply a second crop of wood. Two other physical characteristics existed then as now. Firstly the hills which surround us on every side and from which we derive the first part of our name; and secondly, after heavy and continuous rain, water would cascade down from the Wake Arms area and cause flooding.

And so we move on 100 years to 1166, and to show what can happen in such a period of time, I will digress and describe what has happened in the last 100 years of this Century say from 1890-1990. Firstly there were no motor vehicles or aeroplanes in 1890, but these modes of transport have now reached a high degree of sophistication. We have radio, television, microwave, electronics, computers, satellites and man has travelled in space and set foot on the moon. So what happened during the first 100 years of Norman Rule? A great deal, and in particular this massive Survey of the whole country, and preparation of the Domesday Book. But there is nothing to show that anything of special significance happened here, and the forest would pursue the even tenor of its way as it did 100 years previously!. Indeed it was not until we were well into the 13th

An oak tree on the Green in its natural state and shape

One of the avenue trees savagely mutilated so that it bears no resemblance to an oak

Century, that we know anything definite, and this occurred more than a mile from this spot! A big house stood approximately where the present Theydon Hall now stands, and close by an old wooden Church, which we are told was given in 1253 to the Canons & Priors of St. Bartholomew Priory West Smithfield, by one William de Bosco; and I think this is as good a time as any to mention the origin of our Village name. Quite simply we do not know, and therefore what follows are the conclusions myself and some others have arrived at.

Firstly the word 'don' undoubtedly refers to the hills which surround us on every side, and anyone conversant with the old Essex vernacular, will know that the word 'they' also did duty for these, them, and those, which words were not in their vocabulary! In this light 'They Dons' begins to make sense. One thing is generally agreed upon, and that is the word Theydon is much older than the Bois which follows it. So how did we come by this? Here again there is general agreement that the name derived from a family or person, and not from any physical characteristic. One wonders if the old Boyce family believed to have lived in these parts occupied the old Theydon Hall and gave their name to the Village. Alternatively it can have been derived from de Bosco! Whatever its origin one fact stands out, that of the half dozen or so different spellings of the word, *phonetically* all sound alike: I shall refer to this subject later in the book.

But we must return to our ancient Church, which with the Hall is thought to have been in existence a great many years before de Bosco made his gift. There is a record of one of two Rectors who were in office before 1253 and several afterwards. These latter must have been appointed by the Priory, but this plan did not continue, and for the next 200 odd years a monk travelled from the Priory each weekend to take services in the church. Leaving Smithfield on the Friday afternoon he would make his way through the streets of London on horseback and arrive at Leytonstone by evening, where he would stay the night at an inn, possibly where the Green Man now stands. You may

The River Roding in flood, an all too common sight

This picture serves to illustrate how the English Elm established itself on the Village Green

The last English Elms on the Green. These survived until about 1960 when they were considered unsafe and were felled

well ask why he didn't do the journey in one day. There are several reasons for this. If he had done so it would have been dark before he reached his destination, with the countryside getting more wild and inhospitable the farther he travelled, so he could easily have missed his track or be attacked by footpads and robbed or even worse! At the Inn he would learn if the River Roding was in flood and impassable at Woodford Bridge and Abridge. Also at Leytonstone stood, and probably still stands the ancient High Stone which marks the division of the two roads, the Lower Road passing through Woodford Bridge, Chigwell, and Abridge on the way to Ongar, and the High Road via Wanstead, Woodford Green and Loughton to Epping, though the latter was not much better that a track through the forest in those days. So he might decide to take the High Road and approach the Hall from the west. Arriving, a room would be placed at his disposal, and he would return on the Monday, only stopping for a meal en route.

It is unfortunate that there is no information about this little settlement, but much can be gleaned from circumstantial and environmental details. Firstly, nobody is going to build a church, unless the needs of a community demand it, and this little church, now with a Chancel added, looks as if it could accommodate at least 60 souls. So where did the congregation come from? There would first of all be the Master his family and relations, and the domestic staff for the big house. A groom to look after the horses who might also have a family. Then they would have to produce their own food, so a large vegetable garden and orchard would be needed and a staff to maintain it. Finally a farm to supply all the usual dairy products, meat, fowl, and grain, and of course men to work it, for we know with certainty that the land was under cultivation from very early times, because of the road layout. Anyone living who knew the old Abridge Road before 1938, will remember it was not much wider than a cart track, with four sharp right-angle corners near Theydon Hall.

There are a great many roads in Essex which began their life as cart tracks round fields of crops, and which the early traveller on foot would follow. Perhaps the most notorious of these was the road between Ongar and Chelmsford, which had so many sharp corners, that it has taken almost the whole of this century to iron them out! The Abridge Road round Theydon Hall was one of such, and which persisted until the major rebuild in 1938. Much can be learned from roads if we study them. The road between Waltham Abbey and Theydon Bois winds about a great deal, and this can be explained because early travellers on foot would have to detour to avoid such obstacles as ponds, boggy ground, hillocks, and impenetrable thickets.

But to return to our little settlement at Theydon Hall, which seems to have carried on with the Priory supplying Clerics until the 16th Century, when this arrangement came to an abrupt end because of the dissolution of the monastries by Henry VIII.

Now at this time there lived in these parts a certain Edward Elrington, possibly in the big house itself, and the little church which had been given all those years ago to Saint Bartholomew's Priory by William de Bosco, was now handed to Elrington with tithes by King Henry. So the church which had been for so long under the jurisdiction of the Pope, now became part of the Church of England with the King at its head, and from then on the roll of incumbents is fairly complete.

And so we move on to the reign of Queen Elizabeth I, which was probably the most romantic period of our history! We are told King Philip of Spain sought her hand, no doubt hoping to become King of the two Principalities, but nothing came of it, instead he was furious when his ships, laden with booty from the Americas were attacked and plundered by English sailors who even followed them into port. These actions caused him to build his famous (or infamous) armada to invade England. When news of this reached the Queen she set about increasing her navy to combat this menace, and to do this she needed lots of oak to build her ships.

The Bull Inn

Baldocks Farm House 1908

The last of the old cottages in Poplar Row and facing the Green. As it was when Horace Carter lived there.

Parsonage Farm

For a long time I have wondered why the house which now is part of our Bull Inn, together with a handful of cottages were built, as it were, in the middle of nowhere, when the Village community with its church was over a mile away. Perhaps the following suggestion is the answer! As I mentioned earlier in this work, an oak tree needs light and space to grow to its full size, and therefore the best trees would be on the fringes of the forest. So these cottages might have housed the woodmen, with the Supervisor living in the house. It is significant too, that a large area of the forest which includes our Village Green and the Plain, has at sometime been cleared of trees, and those which grew on part of the Green in later years were not normal forest trees but English elms! Most of the cottages were built in what we now call Poplar Row and were facing the Green, with two exceptions. They were in a cul de sac just off what is now Theydon Park Road. As I lived in one of them for almost 5 years, I am able to give first hand details of its construction.

These were Crossgreen Cottages and probably belonged to the farm of that name. They were 'semi detached' and the framework was entirely of hewn hornbeam. To this was nailed rather crude laths, and the whole was plastered over. The floor was what is generally known as a stone floor, probably of small stones and lime and the roof was covered with small rather crude clay tiles. Originally there was only one room up and downstairs, though a scullery had been added much later. The upstairs floor which consisted of oak planks about 2 feet wide and two inches thick were supported by a massive oak beam which straddled the downstairs ceiling. The only brickwork was the chimney stack which served both houses. There was a small porch over the front door supported by two pillars of oak in their natural state. These two houses were pulled down when the Pakes Estate was built. They had no foundations.

As I have lived and worked in this area for 65 years, and most of which time I spent at the Garage, I naturally took especial interest in this spot. Over the years I have done some research regarding the land hereabouts, and though information is sparse,

No. 1 Cross Green Cottages. This pair of Weatherboard Cottages were not as old as Nos. 3 & 4. The ladies are Mrs. Pede who lived there, and Mrs. Parish grandmother of Harold. I lived at No. 4

I have arrived at certain conclusions which I offer for your consideration. Firstly where were the boundaries of this "Bull House" property? On the West side was and is Epping Forest. On the North there was this deep ditch which drained the watershed as far back as the Wake Arms, and which after heavy and sustained rain would have to cope with a colossal amount of flood water. I think therefore that this would be the natural North boundary. On the East side I would suggest the land between this house and the Parsonage farm was mutually divided more or less equally between the two. Finally on the South side I suspect the land and cottages facing the Green were owned originally by the "Bull House". Even as late as 1938 the Bull Inn owned the land including two houses as far as Pakes Farm. How useful this land would have been today for a Car Park!

I would expect the transition of the Bull from a dwelling house to an inn to be gradual, with the occasional traveller being put up for the night and receiving breakfast before he went on his way. It is obvious too, that because of the deep ditch on the one side and the row of cottages on the other a vehicle would have to use the Bull's private road; and so we hear of the Toll House being erected and a gate spanning the road at the western boundary of the Inn.

As I was told a great deal about this old Toll house by Mr C.H. Wood, and can add my own personal experience, I will write down all I know of this interesting subject.

Of late years it was known as 'the Cabin' and as I owned the property from 1967-1972 I will first give details of its construction. It was built of rather crude bricks with no foundations. It had a brick floor laid straight on the earth. Joists and rafters were all of hewn hornbeam, and the roof was slated. This however was not the original cladding for the starking boards on which the slates were nailed were of a comparatively modern kind. By its construction I would put its age as mid 18th Century, but it could be older.

The Old Toll House later known as the Cabin, where the keeper of Theydon Green Gate lived

One of the oldest houses in Theydon Bois, and certainly the oldest in Theydon Park Road. Believed to have been in existence for 300 years.

Mr. Gussin outside his shop with his dog. After his death his two daughters Sarah and Emily carried on the business trading as S and E J Gossin

The old Alms Houses with two of the inmates by their doors. The two original prints on this page were given me by Annie Glibery who worked at Gussins' shop, and lived to be 100!

The gate keeper is believed to have worked at the Inn and only opened the gate when someone wished to pass through. The east wall of the Cabin was in line with the West boundary of the Inn so that he was in a position to collect tolls before allowing them through the gate.

Mr Wood came to Theydon Bois in the late 1870's as a young man and in 1888 opened a drapers shop on part of the site now occupied by Wood and Krailing's showroom.

The Garage House and the Cabin were at the time owned by Mr George Ketts of Buckhurst Hill and were leased to Mr Wood who continued to hold the lease until his death in 1938. It then passed to his surviving partner George Krailing and was held by his family until I was able to buy the freehold of the Garage, and Jack Cusworth the freehold of the Cabin when the property was put up for auction in 1952. I purchased the Cabin from Mr Cusworth in 1967 when he retired and sold the Garage and Cabin to its present owners in 1972. I am sorry they saw fit to knock the old Toll House down.

As the duties of the Inn increased, it had less and less use for most of the surrounding fields, so much of this land was disposed of in plots for smallholdings.

I read some years ago that the original Birch Hall was a nunnery. If this was so it would have been cleared by the King at the time of the Dissolution. Edward Elrington owned it with certain land in 1578, but he may not have lived there, preferring to be near the church and community for which he was responsible. Birch Hall is two miles from the site of the old Theydon Bois Church and Elrington must have been quite old by 1578! He could I fancy have been classed as Lord of the Manor of his day. A number of eminent people held this title over the years, and would no doubt be chief among the Trustees of the old almshouses built in 1753.

By the turn of the Century, some sort of census must have been taken, for the population in 1801 is given as 334. This on the

The Village Post Office began its existence in 1853 in part of the Old Weatherboard Houses. This picture shows its second site very early in this century

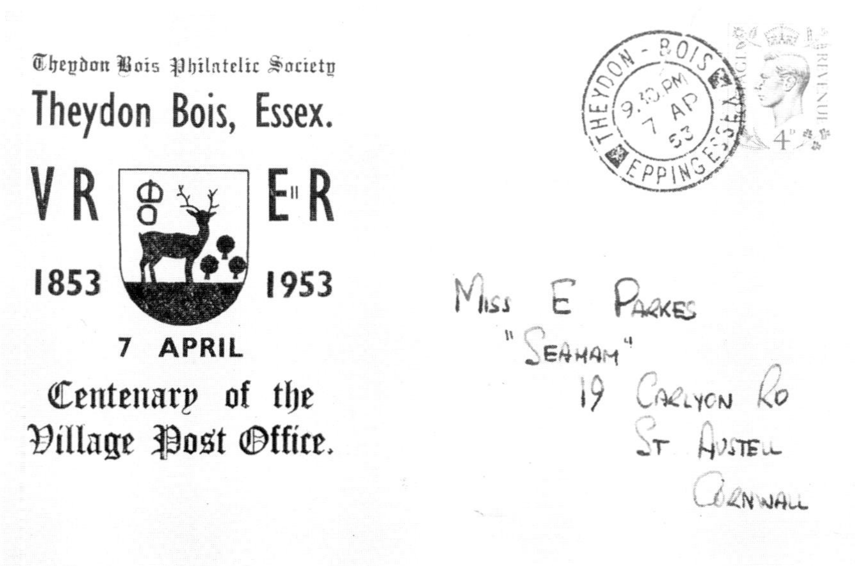

A first day cover to mark its Centenary in 1953, then removed to its third situation in Forest Drive

face of it seems an awful lot of people in a small village consisting almost entirely of farm and forestry workers. But once again we must regard this figure in its proper perspective. The Parish of Theydon Bois begins at Piggots Farm some two or three hundred yards from Abridge, and in those early days any semblance of a road finished here for the River Roding regularly flooded the next strip, and it was not until 1857 that some sort of road was made over what we all knew as Abridge Washway. In a westerly direction the Parish of Theydon Bois extended and still extends almost to the Wake Arms. Beginning with the Boundary of Loughton Lane, the Ancient parish included Bell Common and that part we know as Ivy Chimneys, and the Parish contained as many as fifteen farms. We must also remember it was customary to have large families in those early days (my grandparents had eight and nine respectively), so this number of 334 might only have consisted of 30 or 40 male adults!

I think at this stage of my story, I should relate how the Farm labourer lived in those early days, when there was no Gas, Electricity, Piped water, or Sewerage facilities. Most of the cottages had a large graden where fruit and vegetables were grown sufficient to last through the Winter months. Some plants like cabbage, celery, and parsnips could be left in the ground until required, others including potatoes and apples would be stored away from the frost. Jamming, pickling, and drying were also resorted to. Milk, butter, and eggs could be obtained from the farm, though some cottagers might keep fowls. For meat: ducks, chickens, geese, and even pigeon and sparrows made into pies! But the real meat supply was the pig. These were fattened to about 25 stone and killing began from September onwards. If there were a number of families 3 or 4 might share a pig, and three such groups would each kill their pig in turn so fresh meat would be available up to Christmas. But the bulk of the carcass was pickled with salt and the great flitches were hung from the pantry ceiling beams, meat being cut off as required until the following April, but not later, as the meat tended to become rancid. This was the origin of the old saying that one should never eat pork unless there was an R in the month!

The best lighting was by oil lamp burning paraffin, and there were some really fine examples. Otherwise illumination was provided by tallow candles and rushlights, this last being a rather unsatisfactory crude affair, always flickering, but had to be used when there was nothing else available.

Washday was always Monday, and it was considered very bad management to wash later in the week, as the following little rhyme points out. It was taught my mother when a girl.

> Those who wash on Monday have all week to dry,
> Those would wash on Tuesday if things had gone awry;
> Those who wash on Wednesday have but themselves to blame,
> And those who wash on Thursday wash for very shame;
> Those who wash on Friday wash for very need,
> And those who wash on Saturday are very sluts indeed!

All the cottages would have a copper where the clothes were boiled, but how the women got their washing so sparkling white using yellow Sunlight soap, Hudson's soap powder, Reckitts Blue, and starch beats me! Here is another old song about washday and what followed. It was called 'Dashing away with a Smoothing Iron'.

> Twas on a Monday morning when I beheld my darling,
> She looked so neat and charming in every high degree;
> She looked so neat and nimble O, a-washing of her linen O
> Dashing away with a smoothing iron she stole my heart away.

There were seven verses. On Tuesday it was a-hanging out her linen-O; on Wednesday a-starching; on Thursday a-ironing; on Friday a-folding; on Saturday a-airing; and on Sunday of course she was a-wearing of her linen-O.

One day a week was set aside for baking, and on this day enough bread was made to last the week-out. And it was excellent bread although often baked in a very primitive oven.

As it was in the beginning . . . . . .

Is Now . . . . . .
These seats could tell a good tale, not least their help in increasing the local population!

The 'Loo' was down the garden. It had a wooden seat with a hole cut in it and the soil was kept reasonably sweet and dry with quicklime. There was a flap at the back so that the stuff could be shovelled out when full and thrown on the manure heap. At my Grandmother's little farm at Epworth in Lincolnshire there were two holes side by side on the seat, and I took some convincing as a young lad that two occupants didn't perform together!

For clothing and boots and shoes, one had to walk to a large town such as Romford, unless able to cadge a lift on a waggon taking a load of hay or straw into London for the horses, or cattle brought into Smithfield abattoir by the drovers.

Early in the 19th Century, the Hall-Dare family owned the Manorial rights of our Village, and the son of the Lord of the Manor, Lieutenant Hall-Dare R.N., having been left a legacy, wished to use it to benefit the Parish in some way. He decided to plant the avenue of oak trees across the Village green, and it is reported that the holes were dug by his father's workmen, and after a lunch at the Bull Inn with his friends, the trees were duly planted. Why he needed this legacy to pay for this exercise when he got his labour for nothing, and could find plenty of young oak trees growing on the Estate I can't imagine, and I thought he must have spent his money on the wrought iron seats which graced our Avenue for many years. However the forest authorities *think* the seats were given to the Corporation in 1900. If this is so they must have been secondhand, for I am certain they were much older than that. It is significant too, that the Hall-Dare family sold their Manorial rights to Gerald Buxton in 1900 so the seats may have been their parting gift. Most readers will be aware that I spent 6 months last year restoring four of these seats, and a number of things I noticed during the work convinced me they were much older than the suggested 90 years. Recently another wrought iron seat has come to light buried deep under a huge blackberry bush. This is entirely different from the four I restored and it will be extremely difficult to do because I have no pattern and much iron work is damaged

An early photograph of Mr. Gerald Buxton of Birch Hall, Theydon Bois, which he had erected between 1891 and 1894. He could justifiably be considered the last Lord of the Manor of this village

The Old Theydon Bois School built in 1840 now occupied by The College of Preceptors

The new Village Primary School built and opened in 1959

The Old Weatherboard Houses with the little converted Cricket Pavilion in the distance

The scene as it is today with its row of new shops

Loughton Lane early this Century

The same as it is today

Woburn Avenue about 1910. Just about all the working class population lived here in rented accommodation. No-one could afford a car

Woburn Avenue today. Only a very few of the old residents remain and most everybody owns a car

or lost. All these seats were in a shocking state of disrepair and there is still a possibility that one or two of the originals ended up in the scrapyard. All these seats were damaged and broken as far back as 1927 when I first came to Theydon Bois, and it is a miracle that most of them have survived to this day. It is worthwhile mentioning that every one of the oak trees planted by Hall-Dare took root and prospered, whereas those along the green by what we know as Chapel Road were a failure because, only three survived. They were intended to mark the Silver Jubilee of King George V! By the time Hall-Dare planted his trees, one would expect that the old weatherboard cottages in the High Road together with some Farm houses were in existence.

By 1840 the population had increased to about 500, and the new School was built, and administered by the Church. With the Old Church so far away, some thought was now given to building a new one more central to where most of the people were now living. In 1842 the Rev. George Hambledon became the incumbent, with the title of Perpetual Curate, when it was decided to build a new Church on high ground conveniently near the Epping Road and what we now call Coppice Row.

Because much has been written over the years about this subject, I do not propose to give a full account, but just an outline of events. I shall nevertheless make a few observations.

Briefly then, the new Church was built on the present site, and consecrated in 1844, but by 1850 it was considered unsafe due mainly to inadequate foundations, and was demolished. The speed at which the demolition was carried out, the strengthening of the foundations, and the building of the present Church all in a period of 6 months, takes one's breath away, and shows dedication of a very high order!

Regarding the old Church at Theydon Hall which was pulled down in 1844, I am led to wonder if the Tower was first dismantled to make it easier to remove the bells for the new Church, and afterwards nobody was interested in rebuilding it, so the church itself was pulled down and the materials sold for £78.00. This money would help pay for the new church.

What happened to the Communion Vessels and Altar furniture is not known, and one wonders why they were not transferred to the new Church. Perhaps those who took down the Church and paid the £78.00, considered they belonged to them! Certainly none of the items have ever been found.

In 1856 the Eastern Counties Railway built their branch line from Stratford to a terminus at Loughton where Brown's Garage now stands. Shortly afterwards some influential people in Epping formed a sort of consortium to promote a line from Epping to connect with the Loughton Branch. However, before they were able to do so the Eastern Counties Railway had absorbed a number of smaller railways, and a new company was formed with the more grand title of the Great Eastern Railway.

John Windus the Epping lawyer had been plagued for years by the variations in the spelling of the Theydon Village name. Since he had been appointed Town Clerk for the Epping Parish Council, the problem had become more acute, but he had done nothing about it. He had been acting for the promoters of the proposed line to Loughton, and now in front of him was a letter from the Great Eastern Railway whose representative was calling that morning to discuss certain queries, one of which was how they should spell the name on the new Theydon Station. At the meeting the spelling Bois was decided upon as it seemed the most appropriate in view of the large amount of woodland in the area. Thus the Railway stabilized the spelling for all time.

I suppose the coming of the Railway caused the biggest upheaval in our Village that it has ever suffered. Opened in 1865 and terminating at Ongar it divided the Village into two parts! The general public who had been in the habit of crossing from West to East and East to West at practically any point they chose, now found their way barred by a fence, with a 'notice' "Trespassers will be prosecuted", with a £5.00 fine for

With the coming of the railway, level crossing gates controlled road traffic. Wicket gates were provided for pedestrians who could cross the lines at their own risk

A crowd of East-Enders waiting for their excursion train to pull in off the spur

infringement! This was a lot of money in those days, and much more than the average labourer would earn in a month! The frustration of having to walk the best part of a mile along the Railway boundary to an official crossing place, and then back on the opposite side to reach a point a few hundred yards as the crow flies from where they started can well be imagined.

Although by now the old Green Gate had gone, we had instead, level crossing gates under the control of the Railway. Pakes Farm which was owned by Debenhams of Thrifts was almost completely cut off from its pasture, and the old Cow Bridge wide enough to take a horse and cart had to be erected before the spoil could be removed from the cutting. Towards Loughton the Railway had cut through another large field leaving a strip of land about 200 yards wide on its western flank. Over the years this strip was sold off in plots by either the Railway or as seems more likely the person to whom they sold it. The Railway had also to put in an uncontrolled level crossing about ¼ mile south of the cow bridge because they had isolated a solitary house on the East side of the line. There was only one other crossing point in the Parish which was the footpath between Parsonage Farm and the old Mission Hall at Ivy Chimneys.

Having dealt with the physical changes to our Village brought about by the Railway, we can now examine the effects it had on the population. The first and obvious thing was that they now had easy access to the large towns, and to the Metropolis itself. Then the Railway offered jobs with better pay and conditions, a uniform provided, privileged travel on the line, chances of promotion, and a job for life if they behaved themselves. So it was that a number of men left farming and forestry and took jobs with the new concern.

The next change brought about, was the very easy access of East Enders to visit us. It is true they had visited Epping Forest for years travelling by the horse-drawn brakes, but these were slow and much of the time was spent travelling, so most got no further than High Beach. Now the journey to Theydon Bois

Early this Century. Train of old type coaches to Liverpool Street (The land on which Theydon Bois Station stands was purchased from three separate smallholders, and that of the goods yard from a fourth)

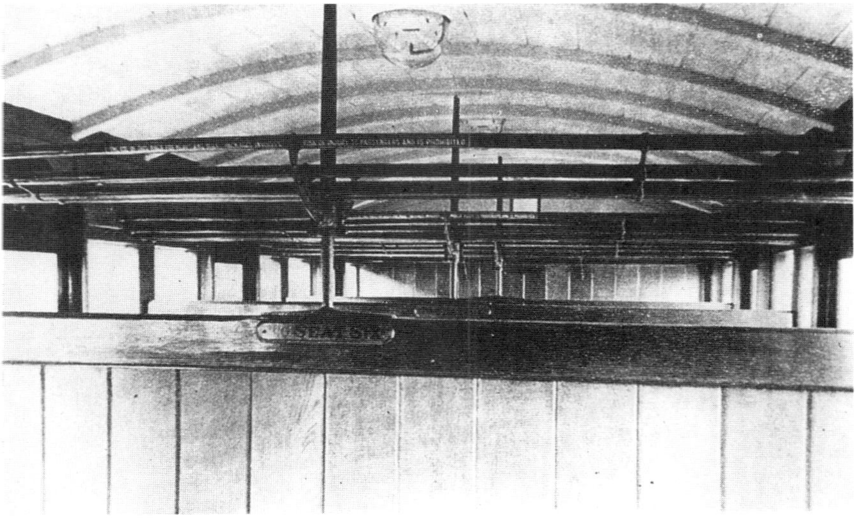

Shewing the Spartan open top carriages used by the Great Eastern

Horse drawn brakes outside the Wake Arms

Dossett's Retreat after its removal from the Green to Coppice Row. Later taken over by William Gray.

Riggs Retreat in its heyday, after it was taken over by Teddy Yates

Both Retreats destroyed by a German parachute mine at 3.36 am precisely November 18th 1940.

took no longer than 45 minutes, and even less if they came on a special excursion train. These trains could carry as many as six or seven hundred adults and even more children! So they came in their hundreds and once the train had disgorged its load, the carriages were left in the spur alongside the up line ready for the return in the evening.

These people had to be "fed and watered", and so the Retreats came into being. Mr Dossett who owned a lot of the land hereabouts opened a Retreat opposite the South West corner of the Green on part of the land where John and Doug Gooch live. He soon found that most of the East Enders streaming off the trains were walking straight up the road towards the Forest, so he removed his Retreat to a site in Coppice Row, which was eventually acquired by William Gray, and built a row of houses on the old site which he called Chestnut Cottages and which he rented to local people.

It did not take the Riggs family long to realise the potential of Theydon Bois. They already had several other Retreats in various places, and now began to build one in Coppice Row a little farther up the hill than Grays, but on the opposite side of the road. Each Retreat had a Roundabout and various amusements and sideshows, but their most important function was to feed the visitors. Between them Grays and Riggs could feed 5,000 to 6,000 people at one sitting. The Retreats were built entirely of wood and were two storeys high, many of the meals being served upstairs. Some regular employment was found for the Villagers, and any amount of part-time work in the season.

But it was not only the East Enders who were attracted to our Village. A number of wealthy people wished to settle here now they could get to the City easily and quickly. So in 1870 the Villas on Piercing Hill were started and completed about two years later. Most of the moneyed people lived here, but there were also about 6 large houses elsewhere in the Village. The last Birch Hall was built in 1892, but that has now gone. These big houses needed domestics, coachmen, and gardeners and so the variety of jobs available to the villagers widened. I think now I had better deal with the Woburn Avenue and Blackacre Estates, for there was much activity in this area from 1885 onwards. Woburn Avenue was always known locally as the Port Wine Estate because it was said that the House agents so primed their would-be purchasers with Port Wine, that they didn't realise what they were signing! Most of the working class population lived here, renting the property from the owners. Mr Dossett even owned some of the houses in this road!

Blackacre Farmhouse is said to have dated back to the 17th Century and I am informed that the road from the corner of the Green to the farm was called Crofton Lane, and this presupposes that the name was taken from an early occupier of the farm and farmhouse. The name is perpetuated in the house Crofton Lodge which was built on the alignment of the lane before Theydon Park Road was cut.

I must now relate what happened to my Uncle, Charles Farmer when he worked for Goulds of Loughton. Goulds farmed most of Maitlands land and possibly some of their own. But they were also Corn Chandlers selling fodder, seed grain and implements to other farmers. They also had a number of shops in the immediate districts where one could buy oats, wheat, maize, bran, middlings, dog biscuits, vegetable seeds, pigeon mixture and even garden tools. Charles drove one of their heavy waggons hauled by a pair of shire horses.

So it was that one winters morning he had to deliver fodder and grain to Blackacre Farm. There had been a great deal of rain and somewhere about where Hill Road now is his waggon sank down to the axles in the mud. After carrying sacks of corn weighting 1½ cwts on his back to the farm along with bales of linseed cake for the cattle he had to offload the rest of his goods before the horses could shift the now empty waggon. He never forgot it and was the only person I ever knew who disliked Theydon Bois and in particular Blackacre Farm.

Hill Road in the thirties. On the left is the 18th Century Blackacre Farm House, sadly it was demolished when houses were built on the east side after the last war.

Hill Road as it is today, now kerbed and metalled.

Crofton Lodge; built on the original alignment of Crofton Lane in 1876

Blackacre Road in the thirties.

At the bottom of the hill and just short of where the Kitsons live a road branched off to the left which gave access to Crossgreen Cottages. This was of course long before the Kitsons house was built which I am informed was erected in 1907. It was originally called the Corner House because Theydon Park Road eventually passed its other frontage. We know there was a Crossgreen Farm but I have no knowledge as to where it was though one would expect the cottages belonged to it. By the number of ancient pear and apple trees in the gardens of Theydon Park Road one is led to wonder whether it was a fruit farm.

When Theydon Park Road was eventually made it deviated considerably to the left of the old Crofton Lane leaving a sort of triangular bit of no mans land in front of Crofton Lodge, and this appears to have been absorbed over the years leaving this house with a very irregular front garden. On the opposite side the Corner House owned all the land as far as the top of the Hill, but a large piece of the garden was sold off as a building plot by John Lane when he lived there. This road winds about a good deal because the first houses backed on Pakes meadow and afterwards the rest were governed by the Railway boundary. Most of the houses were built in the latter end of the last century or early in this, six at least being owned by the ubiquitous Mr Dossett including the house where I now live. Many of the remaining sites were built upon by Mr Pearce between the wars, and the remainder by various builders since the last war ended.

Blackacre Road had no special characteristics, except it was cut on the steepest part of Blackacre Hill. Many extra houses have also been added in this road since the last war.

When eventually Hill Road was made, its surface was hardened off with Hoggin but was never adopted and metalled until after the last war. Originally all the properties were on the west side but about 1936 Mr Kemp bought a plot at the top of the east side and Ken Lodge (No. 33) was built. After Blackacre Farm

The Old Essex Pet. A bit eccentric but harmless. He could be seen in this area early in the Century. His name was believed to be Spruzen. Other 'Characters' I can remember were Donkey Scott, The Duchess, Top Top Torvey and Peggy Wooden Leg.

House was demolished and the pond filled in, the remainder of the houses on the east side were built.

All the houses built on the Blackacre Estate were for middle class residents, and were erected by various builders, many of whom lived locally, particularly the Gooch and Keen families.

Theydon Park Road terminated at No. 73 because carrying it further would have created problems with the sewerage system. Even so the sewer in Theydon Park Road is in places as much as 15 to 20 feet deep. This is a highly specialised type of engineering on which we depend for our health and well being.

But what of those people who had houses and bungalows, built on the Loughton side of Theydon Park Road, and particuarly those who bought a plot of that strip of land further on?

They had no gas, water, electricity or sewer, though eventually the Water company was prevailed on, possibly by the Sanitary Inspector, to lay in a 2" main, but even this went only as far as 'Ashdene' which stands on the boundary of Theydon Bois and Loughton. There was no road as such and during the winter months and spring rains it was just about impossible to reach there with a vehicle, and if one did they would have the hill to climb to get out! Some improvement was made for those living on the hill when it was hardened with hoggin, though the surface soon became a mass of potholes.

What the people who had purchased plots on that strip of land were told about amenities by the sellers, one can only guess. Many of the purchasers erected little shacks on their sites using the cheap ccorrugated iron as cladding. So it was the settlement became known as Tintown, a name which is still in use today by the old local originals. Some of these were better constructed than others so that the owners not only spent their holidays in them, but would let their friends use them for theirs so they too could enjoy the countryside. Trouble came when some of the residents decided to try to live there all the year round and some of the more adventurous tried to drive their cars down which soon sunk to the axles in the mire giving my Garage all sorts of problems getting them out. Invariably they were not in a position to pay for the service, and after one or two occasions of not being able to get our money, we were forced to demand payment before we even started the job. This often meant using an extremely long length of wire rope as the breakdown vehicle had to stand on hard ground. One could be injured by the whiplash if the cable should break.

From the very first conditions were primitive to the extreme. Even after water was piped as far as 'Ashdene' it was some time before some arrangement was made to supply the end houses with a service pipe supply. Great difficulty was still being experienced for a vehicle climbing the hill even though it had been hardened off.

Paraffin was generally used for heating and lighting by most residents, though a few of the better built bungalows were able to use coal. One wonders how old Charlie Oliver who was brother of Bill Oliver our Coal Merchant, managed to deliver coal to them as he couldn't chance his lorry farther than the bottom of the hill.

In 1928 The County of London Electric Supply brought Electricity to the Village, and this must have been a Godsend to the people in Tintown. When Calor Gas came on the market some years later, and residents were able to cook with gas, things were getting a bit more civilized. But they still had, and even today still have no sewer, and so are left a place down the garden, an Elsan Closet, or going to the expense of installing a modern septic underground tank which can be emptied and disposed of by the Local Authority.

Over the years the residents have hardened off the old track with any hardcore they could procure, so that today vehicles do not get set. But the road is still full of potholes which fill with water whenever it rains. Since the last war the road to

The five o'clock train to Epping approaching Theydon Bois Station, photo by Frank Surridge taken from Old Cow Bridge in the late twenties.

And todays electric train photographed from the same spot.

the bottom of the hill has been adopted with the surface kerbed and properly metalled. The opportunity was used to put in a sewer and has meant installing a sludge pump at the bottom of the hill. Only recently has a Gas main been put in to supply the houses to the extreme end.

As an ex Fire Officer who had been in charge of the local fire protection I had been concerned that there was only one Fire Hydrant at the end of this long road, and at last persuaded the Essex County Fire and Rescue Service Water Officer to install a new one outside 'Rylin' just in time to save the houses after the field caught fire during the dry summer of 1990.

The chapter on the Buxton family in my previous book covers the subject fairly well. However, there are a few additions which should be mentioned. Gerald Buxton had his Birch Hall erected more or less on the original site. The work was begun in 1891 and completed in 1894. In 1900 he purchased the Manorial rights from the Hall-Dare family who had held it a great number of years, but not before the Hall-Dares as patrons had appointed Rev. G. V. Collier as Vicar. He began his ministry in 1901.

You will have heard that the Buxtons were accused by the people of annexing forest land illegally, but old Charlie Maynard the elder brother of Herbert our postman, was always saying the Buxtons had stolen land from the Maynard family. I think he must have been referring to the land at the top of Coppice Row which the Maynards used to cultivate, and probably never was theirs anyway!

We now come to a most interesting part of Theydon Bois' History. It concerns the many farms that exist or have existed in the Parish. Some of these were quite small, possibly 30 acres or less, for one must remember in early days everything was done by hand, and such machinery as there was, was hand operated.

Leaving Abridge, we first arrive at Piggots Farm, which was arable and dairy. Land adjacent to the river was never tilled because of flooding. Conversely it produced some very lush grazing in the spring.

The next is Theydon Hall Farm but before I enlarge on this I must give a short account of the history leading up to its purchase by Whitbreads. The Brewery at Abridge was owned in the last Century by two men in partnership, a Mr Hargreaves and Mr Clements who produced their Abridge fine ales. In 1900 the Business was sold to Whitbreads along with about 10 public houses they owned or leased. The new owners pulled down the old Live and let Live and concentrated their business on the relatively new Railway Arms. Their purchase of the Theydon Hall Farm was primarily for the purpose of breeding the shire horses used to haul the heavy brewers drays over the cobblestone streets of the City of London. Whitbreads were always very kind to their horses and would send them down to Theydon Hall Farm to recoup after months of heavy work. So this stud farm also acted as a convalescent home. I had to visit the farm from time to time to service their Crosley Stationary Engine. The place was always spotless with an air of quiet efficiency. It was managed by Mr C.E. Cullyer father of Mrs Rush with two very able assistants in the persons of Messrs Strickland and Oddy who lived in the cottages on the Abridge Road. Jack Strickland who for many years drove the Lord Mayor's Coach in the Lord Mayors show, began his working life here.

The next farm was Spring House Farm belonging to Robert Hough, and administered by his son Cecil for his mother after Robert had been killed in the Hunting field. It was entirely arable. Cecil looked after this farm along with Hydes which he owned, but this latter is not in our Parish. Cecil's hobby was the breeding of Arab horses and his stables were covered in prize tickets.

The farm at Thifts Hall had a small herd of cattle, looked after by Charlie Furlong who lived in the farm cottage. It is possible that some of the milk produced was supplied to Pakes Farm, as this was owned by Debenhams who lived at Thifts.

In 1927 when I came to Theydon Bois, Parsonage Farm was occupied by Mr Leland Buxton, a relative of Geralds, but I saw very little farming activity, and the big field next to the Station seemed to have been taken over by Thrifts.

Theydon Bois Cricket Club
Victorian style (I wonder where they got those top hats?)

Tug of war at the Fête on the cricket field in honour of King George V Silver Jubilee 1936.

Group of locals outside The Queen Victoria in 1946.

Les Grayling on Wood and Krailing's forecourt 1958.

The insurance company called it 'Act of God' when this huge Elm tree crashed down on Barnes' bakehouse in 1918. In the picture is Mr. Albert Barnes, young Bert Barnes sitting on the rail, Rosie and Emmy standing, with Mr. Smith who worked in the bakehouse.

Ada Waters who for a great many years ran the draper's shop in Coppice Row. Very much respected, she taught in the Baptist Sunday School.

Pakes was our Dairy farm and supplied most of the milk for the Village. It was tenanted by James Giblett, a Somerset man and his family. After the first World War Debenhams put the farm up for sale and it was probably then bought by Giblett. I was given all the literature of the sale some years ago and presented it to the Epping Forest District Museum, Waltham Abbey.

Blackacre Farm was tenanted by three generations of Harry Smiths. In the early days Harry Smith the first had a lot to do with horses and was warned off for cruelty by Mr Wood when a Special Constable. It was a mixed farm and turned over to arable during the last war. It seems a great pity the 17th Century farm house was destroyed.

Nothing much is known about Green Farm except that a Mr F.W. Ryder lived there. But the only piece of land not accounted for is that on the East side of Loughton Lane covering the Hornbeam Estate, Graylands and the Frank Foster Home so it may have been here!

Elm Farm was opposite the Elm Stores on land now used by the council, and would likely have worked the land now occupied by the Cricket field and the Red Oaks Estate, in which case the resident farmer would have been a tenant of Birch Hall. But I can find no details of this.

Baldocks farm house still stands today, and the farm area is now covered by the Baldocks Farm Estate. The farm was mainly arable and owned by Carson who sold it to Horace Morgan, who in turn was able to dispose of it for building land.

Crystalbrook was attached to Bellingham House where Mr Worsley lived. As far back as I can remember there always seemed to be a few horses grazing there, and now of course it is the Crystalbrook Riding School. Part of the large field owned by Mr Worsley was taken over by the Essex County Council when Piercing Hill was re-aligned, and the remainder was purchased by the Epping Forest Conservators with the money they received

Forest Drive about 1938.

And taken from the same spot Forest Drive today.

The old drinking fountain at the top corner of The Green. Though the super structure was removed, the fountain itself survived into the thirties –

– when it was replaced by this very utility example, which only survived until after the War, when it was scrapped altogether.

when they had to give up land near the Waterworks Corner Woodford. This field has been let to Theydon Bois Golf Club enlarging it to 18 holes.

Gregories Farm was arable and dairy, but John Padfield intimated to me he was giving up his herd, but may not as yet have done so.

Birch Hall Farm was attached to Birch Hall and I suspect it was to provide dairy produce to the big house. It was and is a mixed farm.

Finally Oak Hill Farm in Coppice Row, occupied by the Morgan family and up to fairly recently by Sid Morgan, who specialised in pigs. Much of the food he gave them was collected as swill from the big hotels in the West End of London, very early each morning.

Most of these farms are still operational today with changes in method and type to suit present day needs.

Recently a contemporary publication stated that the old public drinking fountain which stood at the N.W. corner of the Green "was removed in 1906 and a standpipe fitted". This is not true as only the superstructure was removed, the fountain surviving until the mid 30's, and there are still a number of villagers who can remember it. It was made of blue-grey Granite and I will give a description of it. It was mounted on a stone plinth and stood about 5 feet high overall. There was a position at either side enabling two persons to use it simultaneously. At each side was a rather ornate brass casting, with a button in the centre which when pressed allowed the water to escape through a small pipe just below. Two heavily tinned iron cups were provided, and these were tethered to the main structure by quite substantial chains. Waste water was collected in a shaped sink below the pipe and ducted through a small brass grating into a pool at the bottom put there for small animals such as dogs. The shape and height of this fountain can clearly be seen in early photographs. About the mid thirties trouble was experienced obtaining parts to replace those worn out with use, and so the fountain was removed and a very utility plain modern one put in its place, from which one drunk from the small vertical jet. There were no cups. After the last war with the Retreats gone, even this was considered unnecessary and was removed. One wonders what happened to the old original fountain.

From time immemorial this Village was had to contend with flood water cascading down from as far afield as the Wake Arms after heavy and sustained rain. For years there was an open ditch continuing behind the old Weatherboard Cottages and then taking a N.E. course to a point just north of Theydon Bois Station. Far out it was, and still is joined by water from the Thames Valley area of the Forest, then on to Garnish Hall and Brook House to decant into the River Roding. In 1865 with the coming of the railway, a culvert was put in to replace the ditch near the Station, where it crossed the line. Railways throughout the country have learned to respect flood water, so they made sure this culvert was adequate. At about this time too, it is believed a culvert was put under the Epping road which previously had to be forded. In 1900 when a lot of sewerage work was done the ditch was piped behind the garage. This culvert was painfully small not more than 15 inches diameter, and though adequate for normal rainfall could not cope with floodwater. So as soon as we had heavy and sustained rain, water poured down the Roadway and behind the shop premises. The Railway Arms cellar was always the first casualty and was soon filled with water. It must have been about 1930 when I first experienced the flooding. I can remember it was on a Wednesday in June, and this brought to light a new hazard. In 1926 we had had four new petrol pumps installed, the petrol for which was stored in underground tanks. Water had seeped through the threads of the filler caps so that we were unable to sell any petrol until the water had been pumped from under the spirit. We eventually overcame this nuisance by using non-separator water pump grease on the threads.

1.

2. These two pictures taken in the Fifties show the worst floods we had experienced up until then.

1.

2. And these two of the floods of June 11th 1982 far worse than anything previously experienced, bottom picture shows Charlie Durley wading away from his submerged car.

In 1935 Soper and Co. built their first four shops in Forest Drive, and the Council diverted the culvert to a distribution point outside where the Magpie Gift Shop now is. This was a serious blunder, for not only were several other pipes decanting into this manhole, but the water now had to turn a right angle so that it could pass behind the shops and eventually flow under the Railway.

In 1955 just as I was about to build my forecourt on the corner of Forest Drive, the Essex County Council intimated that they proposed to put in a second and larger culvert alongside the small one at the back of our premises, and I held up the work until they had done so. This extra pipe only made a bad situation worse, as the manhole filled up even more quickly, which goes to prove the Council had just not understood the problem. Here they missed a golden opportunity to rid the Village of this nuisance once and for all by taking a large culvert straight to where the Railway had built their's to pass under the line. The only problem this scheme would have entailed was crossing Forest Drive, for at the time the remainder of the land they would have had to excavate was in virgin soil. But the idea was not taken up although I took the trouble to suggest it. Instead, in the 60's the massive drainage scheme with huge culverts was carried out. But once again they made the fatal mistake of putting in a sharp turn where the pipe crossed Coppice Row. Retribution came on June 11th 1982 when the culvert became choked with debris at this point and the Village suffered the worse flooding ever, at times as deep as 3 feet and enough to cover the bonnet of some cars. Nothing has been done to prevent a recurrence, so one day it is bound to happen again!

At an interview with Edward (Teddy) Purkiss and Stanley (Dick) Griffiths, Dick, who incidentally was born at the Railway Arms pub, is reported as saying a Police Station stood where Wood and Krailing's forecourt now stands, and that the policeman had the very appropriate name of Coppin!

Now I wouldn't dispute that a house stood opposite the Bull Inn, and that the policeman's name was Coppin, but there are

Frank and Percy Surridge
Theydon Bois Station 1928

Mr. C.H. Wood standing by his three businesses in 1910. The Drapery Business, the Cabin Teashop, and the Motor Shop all suffered severely during the 1914-1918 War.

The Theydon Bois Special Constabulary in World War One. Mr. Wood is third from left second row.

D. G. V. O. 11.

Certificate of Official Recognition granted by the War Office to Voluntary Organizations.

This is to Certify that THEYDON BOIS (ESSEX)

a DISTRICT Association for the administration of all Voluntary Work within the limits set out in the application for recognition, has been registered in the Central Registry, London, and is entitled from this date to all the privileges of official War Office recognition, and may make full use of the words, "Approved by the War Office," in connection with its work.

By Order of the Army Council,

Director-General of Voluntary Organizations.

Scotland House,

New Scotland Yard, S.W.

4th October, 1916.

G. D. 6477 1500 10/16 H W V (P)

The War Office Approval Letter.

two definite errors which I must correct. Firstly this Village has never been able to boast a Police Station. All the Policemen we have had over the years – and I can remember eight of them – have lived in rented accommodation in the Village; Coppice Row, Woburn Avenue, The Green, and on the Pakes Estate. The house in which our present PC Sims lives is the first one built specifically for a Police Officer.

Secondly Wood and Krailing's forecourt has never had a house on it. When Frank Gooch built my forecourt and excavated the holes for the five petrol tanks all the soil removed was virgin soil and had never been previously disturbed. These tanks had to be specially made to fit between that blessed(?) culvert and my road boundary, consequently they had an unusual capacity of about 780 gals each!

As you will gather, after the Railway came to Theydon Bois most of the houses were built between 1870 and the turn of the Century, after which there was a lull, followed by the Great War when no houses were built.

I must now write about events leading up to the Great War and the effect it had on our Village. As most of my information came from my old Garage Boss Mr. C.H. Wood. I must first give a short account of his early life.

Born in 1868 at Buckhurst Hill, he knew Theydon Bois as a boy. After he married he moved into No. 55 Theydon Park Road which he called The Warren on account that his family of four daughters were born there. Opening his drapery shop in 1888 on part of the site now occupied by Wood and Krailing's showroom, he also started a Tally business, selling household goods and clothing on Hire Purchase. He employed George Krailing senior to deliver the goods and collect the instalments, travelling as far afield as Walthamstow in a pony and trap. The Cabin had been occupied by a little grocer but his business folded up, mainly because the Bull Inn was too handy, and he kept popping over to 'have one' when he should have been attending to his business. So the Cabin, which came under Mr Wood's lease, was opened by Mrs. Wood and her daughters as a teashop and confectioners. In 1898 he bought his first motor car and began repairing other people's.

This then was the situation at the outbreak of the Great War when everything seemed set fair for a prosperous future.

The immediate effect of the war was the enlisting of many volunteers, and call-up of the regulars into the forces. This made it difficult for the women left behind to pay their instalments and Mr. Wood lost a lot of money this way. Then people either stopped using their cars, as petrol prices had rocketed – if you could get any, others handed their cars to the Government to be converted into Ambulances, so Mr. Wood earned very little here. Then of course the East End visitors all but stopped coming and the tea shop lost a lot of business. It was the last straw when old George began having epileptic fits, which got worse so that he had to be permanently kept in Brentwood Mental Hospital. The Wood family then moved-out of The Warren and used the residential parts of the two houses. Mr. Wood resorted to cutting down trees for logs at one time, and had the bright idea of blowing up the stumps with gunpowder. He managed this alright, but spent the next few days replacing the glass in people's windows.

'Theydon Towers' was turned into a military hospital and convalescent home for officers, and apparently run by voluntary helpers, for on 14th October 1916 they were granted "approval by the War Office" giving them the right to make full use of the words "Approved by the War Office" and be entitled to all privileges. This document was given me several years ago and I presented a copy to the Essex Record Office.

At the top of Lark Hill and Springhouse Hill an anti-aircraft gun was mounted, with its connected searchlight down Coopersale Lane where the maintenance area now is. The Officers from here, and those from the Towers sufficiently recovered to walk down to the Village, were catered for by the Cabin, and

Theydon Bois Wardens' Post B7 stationed at the Vicarage.

Theydon Bois Fire Brigade and about three quarters of my A.F.S. men.

Col. French taking the salute from the Home Guard and Civilian Services circa. 1943.

Thames Valley Hill. This takes its name from The Thames Valley of Epping Forest at this spot.

tea was charged at 6d per cup to keep it exclusive. This was an exorbitant price for a cup of tea, and the place became notorious with all sorts of tales spread about what went on there.

Mr. Wood became a Special Constable, though none of these were supplied with uniforms but just a cap and arm bands. There are 20 of these in a photograph with Police Constable Bailey, and one wonders what they all had to do besides looking important! One worthy is reported as being so frightened when a Zeppelin airship passed over Theydon Bois he had to go home and change his pants!

Food of course was in short supply and rationed, but I venture to say that Theydon Bois with its many farms would be better off than the Towns, and the villagers would almost certainly be able to supplement their rations with a bit of dairy produce.

With the coming of the Armistice the Village realised with something of a shock how many of its young men had been killed and eventually a war memorial was erected in Coppice Row on church property near the Lych Gate.

When the men returned from the War they were promised 'a land fit for heroes to live in', and the most urgent need was for somewhere to live. And so a Council Estate was built, partly in Loughton Lane, and partly in a second row called Red Oaks Mead. These were good houses but 'extremely utility' with the outer doors just plain boards with a latch and finished with creosote. It is most likely that the ground on which these were built along with the cricket field and allotments were once Elm farmland.

Except for those houses already mentioned, all the organised projects were due to the efforts of Horace Morgan who owned Baldocks Farm. It had always been his wish to see his land developed in an Estate and in the early twenties the road we know as Forest Drive was cut, and this could very well be where the Police House stood. It would have been demolished to make way for the road, and explains why no trace of it exists! Fortescue and Scrooby built seven bungalows and three pairs of semi detached houses up this road and then the firm collapsed.

But Horace didn't give up that easily, and in 1932 sold a strip of land to Epping Rural District Council for a Council Estate. So Buxton Road came into being with houses built by Mewburn of Harlow. I believe the rent at the time was 10/- (50p) per week. Some more sporadic building took place by various builders in Chapel Road and Loughton Lane, and a new Telephone Exchange was erected. Our garage number which was Loughton 254 then became Theydon Bois 254, but was changed to 2254 after the Baldocks Farm Estate became a fact.

A new company was formed called Soper and Co. comprising Bill Soper, Harry Heath, Elizabeth Dearden and of course Horace. Building first began at the extremity of Forest Drive with new roads called Morgan Crescent, The Weind, Heath Drive and Elizabeth Drive (afterwards changed to Dukes Avenue). Building carried on steadily until the outbreak of World War II when all activity ceased, but not before the Farm outbuildings and Soper's timber stock, and some vehicles, were destroyed by a disastrous fire in 1936. During the period between the wars the building of the Baldocks Estate was by far the most important event, for it transformed the Village, and by no means to everyone's liking! It caused a division between the indigenous population and the newcomers when they tried to make changes. This schism was never properly resolved until after the Second World War.

During these inter-war years the Retreats were very busy, the East Enders now arriving in fleets of 'General' omnibuses, and on one occasion about 10,000 in a single day! The annual Parish Party was held at Yates's Retreat, and I was allowed to attend as I worked in the Village, and which I have always regarded as great privilege. The Cricket Club made their annual visit to Guist in Norfolk for a game, with a return match at Theydon Bois, though this ended up more of a day's outing and beano than serious cricket! The football team too were very active,

The night goods with one of these J.15 locomotives at its head, would wake up half Theydon Park Road as it struggled up the bank into Theydon Bois.

A modern electric train set to White City

Theydon Bois provides it's commuters with shelter from the weather.

Epping just leaves their's to get wet!

and the Workmen's Club, situated near where Barnmead entrance is today, was always busy. Here one could play snooker, darts, table tennis etc., with whist drives in the back room. Other activities included the Women's Institute, Horticultural Society, Dramatic Society, and Tennis Club to mention the more important. Dances were held at both Retreats.

In 1937 we began to hear about how to deal with poison gas attacks which made us realise the Government felt we might not be able to avoid a second World War. By 1938 we were exhorted to join one of the A.R.P. services, as Air-raid Wardens. A peacetime Fire Brigade had been formed with the Epping Rural District Council as the Fire Authority. There were just two Brigades Theydon Bois and Harlow to cover 56 square miles of our territory. I was Station Officer in charge here, and we were kept pretty busy, sometimes going into Sawbridgeworth to assist and gain experience.

In September 1939 we were at war with Germany, and those in the Village who had joined the Police War Reserve were immediately placed on full time complemented by a number of part time "Specials". The outbreak of the war made little difference to A.R.P. Services, though the incidence of 'Peacetime type fires' showed a marked increase.

Came Dunkirk and the call for Local Defence Volunteers to help resist Invasion if it materialized. At the initial muster outside the Bull Inn, a great number turned up carrying all sorts of weapons. Shortly afterwards Mr Churchill renamed them Home Guard and, as the threat of Invasion receded, their number settled down to about 24 men. These were extremely well trained and would have given a very good account of themselves if their services had been needed. It wasn't their fault that they had little to do.

Not so the rest of us, for when the Blitz started we were kept extremely busy. I was the only full-time fireman in Theydon Bois, and on one or two occasions my little band of Retained men, with such A.F.S. who might be available, were strained almost to breaking point!

After the War ended, most things were in short supply, and it was some years before clothing, food, and petrol came off the ration. We at the Garage were up to our necks in work, getting cars back on the road, and repairing those damaged by bombs, some of which had lain under debris until the War finished. Apart from the chronic shortage of spare parts we had to deal with two other major headaches. One was rusting sometimes even inside the rear axle; the other was fuel systems choked with the gum left behind when the petrol evaporated. Gradually things got back to some semblance of normal.

There was still much to be done to property damaged or neglected during the war. Those houses which had been temporarily patched up, now had to be properly repaired. Many of the houses in upper Coppice Row were too far gone to repair and so were pulled down, and new houses built. The private Sidney Road which for years had nothing but a wide cinder path, was up graded and kerbed, and the vacant plots built upon. There was so much building during the post-war years that I shall only give a general list. Two new Council Estates, Graylands and Pakes. Four new homes for elderly people including some bungalows in Poplar Row, the Frank Foster home in Loughton Lane, a home in Woburn Avenue, and the Robert Daniels Court. The Baldocks Farm Estate was completed, houses on the east side of Hill Road, and new Estates Hornbeam, Barnmead, Slade End and Theydon Gate. Public buildings included a temporary Village Hall, followed by a new Hall constructed in the early 60's, a new Baptist Church and Hall, and St. Mary's Church Hall.

Over the years the Railway had improved considerably. Trains were reasonably clean and comfortable and always dead on time, except during the sort of 'pea-souper' fog we used to suffer in those days. In 1923 the Great Eastern Railway became part of the London and North Eastern Railway, and the Loughton Branch had 13 sets of 8 coaches each, made up of first, second, and third class carriages. At the time of amalgamation these were new and the best train sets on the G.E.R. suburban system.

In 1935 under a 'new works' programme, plans were made for the Central Line of London's Underground to take over our Loughton Branch, to ease the pressure on Liverpool Street station (L.N.E.R.). The line was to travel underground to a new station at Bethnal Green, connect with the District Line at Mile End so that the old Coborn Road station could be closed, resurface temporarily at Stratford, and then travel underground to a point just short of Leyton station where it would connect with the Loughton Branch. I think most of our residents today wish this had never happened, particularly as all the British Rail suburban services are now electrified, and Liverpool Street Station has been completely rebuilt!

So much for the general picture, we must now examine how these changes affected our Village. First and foremost, the old Level Crossing had to go, and a new viaduct was constructed for the B172 roadway. As this meant considerable alteration to the existing road, the opportunity was taken to build a new road as far as Piggot's Farm, for the old road with its four sharp corners and narrowness, was beginning to be a nuisance, with vehicles often having to reverse to a spot where they could pass each other! It was particularly difficult for the Bus service which now ran between Romford and Epping. That the authorities must have realised a war was inevitable is proved by the Air Raid Shelters which were built under the bridge and are still there today. A new footbridge was erected where the gates had been.

Of the three remaining crossing places, only the old Cow Bridge has survived. The uncontrolled crossing south of this bridge was closed. This was made possible by the simple expedience of buying the house and knocking it down! The footpath from Parsonage Farm was also closed. I think we were a bit slow here, as a footbridge might have been erected. The first Central Line train ran into Theydon Bois Station on September 25th 1949, work on the scheme having been stopped during the War years.

The temporary Village Hall erected at the end of the last war and has only recently been demolished-

The new Village Hall erected 1966.

And what of the train service today? The old steam trains always ran to time, and one would have expected these electric trains to be as good. Such however is not the case. A train when it comes – if it comes – will only carry about half the number of passengers an eight coach steam set could carry. Trains are cancelled, re-routed, terminated short of the advertised station with apparently no reference to the timetable. The latest innovation is to close the Booking Office during the day, so if the ticket machine is giving no change what does one do, as it is an offence to travel without a ticket? Currently much lineside work is going on purported to improve the signalling and possibly run automatic trains. Let us hope things get better!

Now that I have brought my little story up-to-date, it is appropriate that I should reflect on the changes which have taken place in our Village since I first set foot here 65 years ago. A number of housing Estates have come into being, and a great number of houses have been built. We have gained one new Church, two Church Halls and a new and spacious Village Hall, four Old Peoples' Homes, a Telephone Exchange, and a new Shopping Centre. The population has changed dramatically, the Village now in the main being a dormitory Village. Many of the residents leave in their cars or by train early morning, and return in the evening. Some are rarely seen in the Village week-ends, but go off in their cars and do their shopping elsewhere. This habit is causing local traders some concern.

Of the very old buildings, we have lost the Cabin; the old houses in Poplar Row which extended into Theydon Park Road; the old cottage where Mr. Clark our Chimney Sweep lived, and where his daughter Mrs. Surridge now lives on the same site but in a modern house; the four Crossgreen Cottages; Blackacre Farm House; and the old Weatherboard houses which stood where the K supermarket now stands.

Both the Retreats were lost by enemy action, and one is led to wonder if they would have survived to the present day, with people driving further afield in their cars for recreation.

We have lost our old Steam trains, and with them all the Goods traffic, Passenger goods, and Mail we used to enjoy. But we are not plagued with the Level Crossing Gates, and have a modern Viaduct over the Railway.

Nobody will deny that without our Village Green, the Pond and the Avenue of Oak trees, Theydon Bois would be just another mediocre Village. I have recently restored the Avenue wrought iron seats, but am conerned about the trees. Seven of these have been cut down over the years and have not been replaced, and several of the others look rather sick. It is time some of the old roots were stubbed up, the hole filled in with fresh soil and young trees planted. The matter is urgent and immediate as oak trees grow slowly, and if something isn't done we could find ourselves with a very depleted Avenue.

Epilogue

To the residents of Theydon Bois I would say, take good care of the environment of our Village, for it is unique and well worth looking after. During my years at Theydon Bois I have always done all that I could to re-instate grass, propagate trees and restore seats on our Green, but now that I am turned 80 there is not much more that I can expect to do, so I must leave it's care to you who will come after me.

PICTURE GALLERY

Now follows early photographs of personages who live, or have lived in our Village.

How many of these can you identify?

A solution is given on page 100.

1

2

3

4

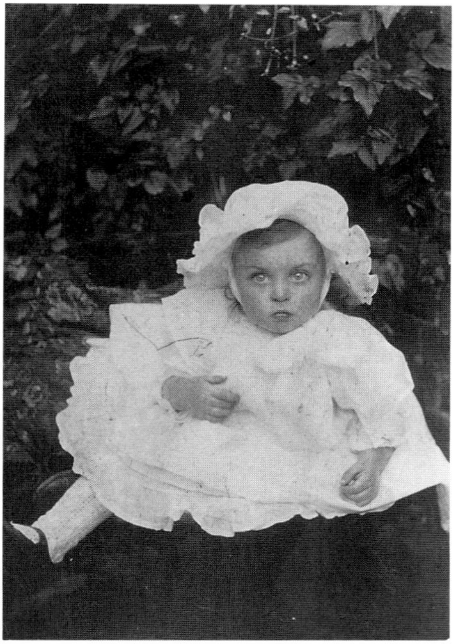

5

6

7

8

9

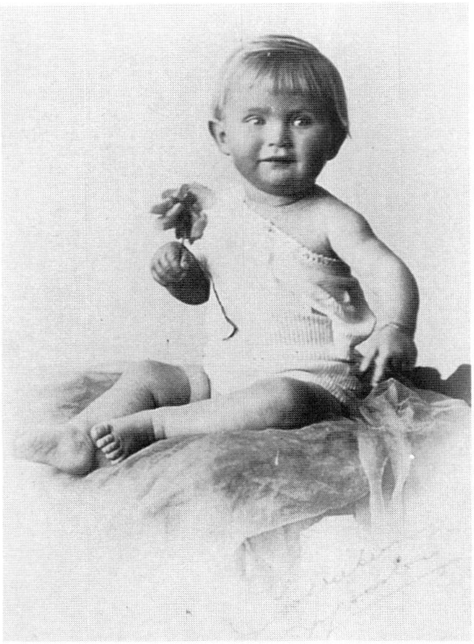

10

11

12

13

14

15

16

17

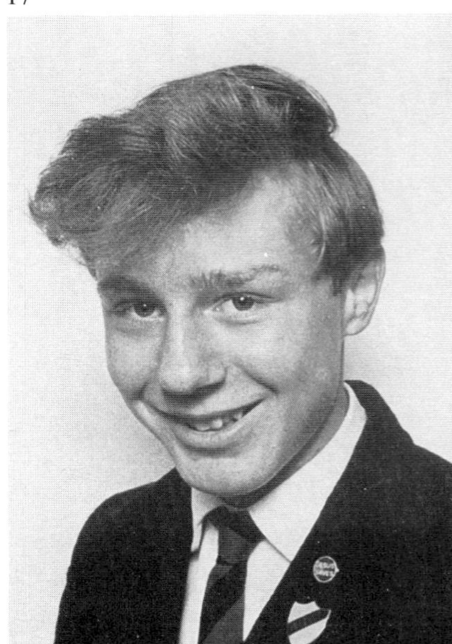

18

19

20

GLOSSARY PART ONE

Glossary Part I

When I first set foot in Theydon Bois some 65 years ago, most of the men and some of the women were always referred to by their nicknames. Sometimes it was years before I found out their proper Christian names, and some are unknown even today.

Here is a list of the old Theydon Bois Originals compiled with the assistance of Frank Surridge

Arthur CONK Andrews
Walter JIM Axon
Bert DOUGHY Barnes
John STRAP OIL Barnes
Walter TITTER Boreham
Chris WITTY Brewer
Edward JIM Brewster
Horace BONNY Carter
Sidney SQUIT Cottee
Harry COVO Coventry
Arthur BUSTER Crabb
Albert GROTNEY Crane
Jim CRACKSON Crane
Robert DANNY BOY Daniels
Colin DINGY Dawkins
George DIXIE Dean
Douglas SQUIBBY Denby
Leonard TUSSACKS Denby
Maurice FATTY Denby
Arthur NIPPER Donald
Muriel MIDGE Donald
Evan John FAIRY Fairchild
John JACK Farmer
Bert DECKER Flack
Walter CON Flack
Walter WAXEY Freshwater
Violet SIS Furlong
Albert DUSTY Furlong
Arthur JOHNSON Furlong
Albert RUSTY Gooch
Valentine PIXIE Gooch
Doris DOT Gooch
Fred DIALLY Gooding
OCCA Gray
Stanley DICK Griffiths
Jack BRUSHER Groves
Basil BAGGY Groves
George BUMMER Gully
Horace PIMPO Halls
DEAFY Halls
George BOSS Halls
Jack BROCKET Halls
Walter POOPY Hughes
Walter HUMMY Hummerstone
Arthur JACKO Jackman
Emrys DICK Jones
Raymond FRITZY Keen
Ethel KACKER Lacey
Harry PEACHY Maynard
Ernest MEL Maynard
Jack TATERS Maynard
William KILLEM Maynard
William BENNY Maynard
Alfred ODZA Mead
Frank DOBBIN Mynott
Harold FETLER Parish

Fred CUTTER Parrish
BANDY Parrish
Charles LARRLY Parrish
William TAFF Patience
George PODGY Patience
Jack NIBBY Poulson
James BUSTER Poulson
SANDY Puffett
Edward NINNY Purkiss
Percy SUCKERS Read
Alfred BUTCH Redgewell
Arthur BANDY Redgewell
Maurice MO Redgewell
George VIMI Redgewell
Tom BROCK Reeves
Chris CODGER Reynolds
Stan COPPER Reynolds
Jim SHAVER Richardson
Jack ROBIN Richardson
Charlie GERRY Rose
JACKSON Saggers
Iris DODDY Sear
Tom CURLY Sear
Harold DANKY Smith
Leonard DARKY Street
William FLAGGY Street
William BRADY Street
Stanley SWOPPER Street
Albert SMUDGY Surridge
Frank TOUGHUN Surridge
Walter BROOMER Surridge
George MOPPER Taylor
Albert THINK-I-DID Thurgood
Jack TIDDLEY Tidd
Violet TWINKLE Twynn
Bertram WEARY Twynn
CURLY Westlake
Alphonso FONZO West
Edward TINKER West
JOCK Wiseman
Charles TALLY Wood
Arthur ROGER Wood
Edward TINDY Wood
George POLLY Wright
Edwin TEDDY Yates
Norah NOBBLER Yates

Even the Church was not exempt!

The Rev E.F.W. Ames was known as STALKY, probably due to his connection with the Boy Scouts. His Church Warden Mr. Gillies who was bald was known as CURLY, and J. Howard Barnes the Lay Reader as HOLY JOE.

Glossary Part II

The origin of some of these place-names is known, some are self explanatory, whilst others are suggested as possibilities and should not be taken too seriously. I have added any anecdotes or scraps of history I have acquired over the years.

ABRIDGE our nearest neighbour, and which name is self-explanatory. The Village ancients would always relate to newcomers how the Winkle Barges came up the river to unload at Abridge.

BLAKE HALL It's railway station was named after the actual Hall which was the seat of the Capel-Cures.

BELL COMMON Takes its name from the Bell Hotel. This area was once part of Theydon Bois Parish.

BUCKHURST HILL The Hill on which most of the Village stands is much higher than Loughton. It's name together with the Roebuck and Bald Faced Stag hotels reminds us of Epping Forest and the deer.

CHIGWELL AND CHIGWELL ROW Birthplaces of my ancestors. Chigwell Church and the King's Head Inn made famous in Dicken's Barnaby Rudge.

COOPERSALE Was this where the men lived who made the casks for the old Epping Brewery? And does the name refer to the ale they drank or the barrels they sold?

CHINGFORD Self explanatory. Fording of the River Ching.

EPPING This name might be the present participle of a verb to 'EP'. One wonders that if we could go back far enough in time whether there was once a forestry process known as epping!

HIGH BEACH Takes its name from the gravelly ground opposite the King's Oak public house. The poor of Loughton would take their children for a picnic there on a Summer Sunday afternoon. The name has no connection with Beech trees!

HALLSFORD BRIDGE Suggests the Hall family crossed the river at this point before the bridge was erected.

IVY CHIMNEYS A self-explanatory name. One time part of Theydon Bois Parish.

LOUGHTON and Lopping Hall. Forever connected with the Commoner's right to lop trees. Their 'Village Hampden' in the person of John Willingale stood up for his rights against the Maitlands and was imprisoned for his efforts.

PASSINGFORD BRIDGE Name suggests that the bridge was some distance from the ford which survived some years after the bridge was built.

ROYDON, RYEHILL, AND RYE HOUSE Roydon Village reputed to have taken its name from the hill and the Rye upon it. Why it should have this connection with Rye which is usually sown on poor soil isn't known.

NORTH WEALD AND SOUTH WEALD Are self explanatory and complementary. North Weald is well known for its aerodrome. The name Bassett to give it it's full name refers to an early de Bassett family.

SNARESBROOK A possibility that animals were snared for food when they went to drink.

STANFORD RIVERS Believed to refer to the stepping stones placed in the shallows. The Essex pronounciation STUNFORD could easily have corrupted to Stanford.

SEWARDSTONE Suggests Anglo Saxon origin.

WALTHAM ABBEY, WALTHAM HOLY CROSS and WALTHAMSTOW all take their name from the great Waltham Forest. The Holy Cross is of course where the body of Queen Eleanor rested on her way to the capital.

WOODFORD BRIDGE The oldest part of Woodford. There was a bridge crossing the Roding in 1777 but it was only a footbridge for pedestrians, animals and carts still using the ford, but by 1816 a bridge for vehicles had been erected.

GLOSSARY PART THREE

Glossary Part III

This is a list of Cockney Rhyme Slang in common use when I was a lad, particularly in the local Brickfield. Naturally it found its way to our Village by the East Enders. Inevitably some of these describe intimate parts of the human body, but to leave them out would have given a totally wrong description of the old London Cockey. Sometimes only part of the slang was used such as "I'm going up the frog", or "Let's have a butchers", which would confuse the uninitiated even more. It is recorded that the German interpreters of the First World war who were sent to interrogate a batch of prisoners, were quite unable to understand what they were talking about, and you may be sure they received no help whatsoever from the Londoners.

ADAM AND EVE – BELIEVE
AIRS AND GRACES – BRACES
ANNA MARIA – FIRE
APPLES AND PEARS – STAIRS
ARISTOTLE – BOTTLE
ARSE AND HOLE – SOUL
AUNT ELLA – UMBRELLA

BALL OF CHALK – WALK
BAND OF HOPE – SOAP
BARK AND GROWL – TROWEL
BARNET FAIR – HAIR
BEECHAMS PILL – HILL
BEES AND HONEY – MONEY
BILLY GOAT – COAT
BIRD LIME – TIME
BLOWER AND HONE – PHONE
BOPEEP – SLEEP
BOTTLE AND GLASS – ARSE
BRISTOL CITIES – TITTIES
BRUSSEL SPROUTS – SCOUTS
BULL AND A COW – ROW
BUSHEL AND PECK – NECK
BUTCHERS HOOK – LOOK

CAIN AND ABEL	–	TABLE
CAT AND MOUSE	–	HOUSE
CHINA PLATE	–	MATE
CHINGFORD HATCHES	–	MATCHES
CLOD HOPPERS	–	COPPERS
CLOTHES PEGS	–	LEGS
COCK LINNET	–	MINUTE
CORNS AND BUNIONS	–	ONIONS
CURRANT BUN	–	SUN OR SON
DAISY ROOTS	–	BOOTS
DICKORY DOCK	–	CLOCK
DICKY BIRD	–	WORD
DICKY DIRT	–	SHIRT
DICKY HANTS	–	PANTS
DIG IN THE GRAVE	–	SHAVE
DIRTY TYKE	–	BIKE
DUCKS AND DRAKES	–	FAKES
EAST AND WEST	–	VEST
FISHERMAN'S DAUGHTER	–	WATER
FOUR BY TWO	–	JEW
FOURTH OF JULY	–	TIE
FROG AND TOAD	–	ROAD
GERMAN BAND	–	SAND
GIVE AND TAKE	–	RAKE
GOD FORBID	–	KID
GRUMBLE AND GRUNT	–	CUNT
HALF INCH	–	PINCH
HAMPSTEAD HEATH	–	TEETH
HAMPTON WICK	–	PRICK
HARRY RANDALL	–	HANDLE
HARRY TATE	–	GATE
HOBBLE DE HOY	–	BOY

JACK JONES – ALL ALONE
JAM JAR – CAR
JIMMY RIDDLE – PIDDLE
JOANNA – PIANO
JOE BLAKE – CAKE
JOHNNY HORNER – CORNER

KATE AND SIDNEY – STEAK AND KIDNEY
KHYBER PASS – ALT FOR ARSE
KING WILLIAM THE THIRD – TURD

LEG OF PORK – FORK
LINEN DRAPER – NEWSPAPER
LOAF OF BREAD – HEAD
LORD LOVELL – SHOVEL

MINCE PIES – EYES
MOTHER HUBBARD – CUPBOARD
MUTT AND JEFF – DEAF

NELSON EDDY – READY (MONEY)
NORTH AND SOUTH – MOUTH

OBADIAH – ALT FOR FIRE
OIL RAG – FAG

PEAS IN THE POT – HOT
PEN AND INK – STINK
PIGS EAR – BEER
PLATES OF MEAT – FEET
PLYMOUTH ROCK – COCK
POLLY FLINDERS – CINDERS
POT AND PAN – MAN
PRUSSIAN GUARDS – CARDS

RAMBLER ROSE – NOSE
RASPBERRY TART – HEART
RICE CAKES – CHRIST'S SAKE
RORY O'MOORE – DOOR

ROSIE LEE	–	TEA
ROYAL BLUE	–	TRUE
RUB A DUB DUB	–	PUB
SKIN AND BLISTER	–	SISTER
SKY ROCKET	–	POCKET
SWEENEY TODD	–	SQUAD
SWEET PEA	–	PEE
TATERS IN THE MOULD	–	COLD
TEA LEAF	–	THIEF
THREEPENNY BITS	–	TITS
TILBURY DOCKS	–	SOCKS
TIN TACK	–	THE SACK
TIT FOR TAT	–	HAT
TOM TIT	–	SHIT
TROUBLE AND STRIFE	–	WIFE
TWO AND EIGHT	–	STATE
UNCLE NED	–	BED
UNION JACK	–	BACK
VEGETABLE MARROW	–	WHEELBARROW
WHISTLE AND FLUTE	–	SUIT
WOOLWICH PIERS	–	EARS
YOU AND ME	–	ALT FOR TEA

I found a tiny sapling growing from the stump of one of the original trees in Poplar Row on the day of my wife's funeral August 23rd 1978. From it has grown the fine specimen of a Lombardy Poplar, important because it springs from the original stock

There are four different species of Poplar Tree in Poplar Row!

SOLUTION TO PHOTOGRAPHS IN THE PICTURE GALLERY – TITLES HAVE BEEN OMITTED

1. Sarah Gussin
2. Emily Gussin
3. Judith and Jennifer Trimby
4. Jack Farmer
5. Harold Parish
6. Albert (Rusty) Gooch and Mrs. Gooch
7. Alan Griggs
8. Rupert Gooch
9. Joy Wainwright
10. Edward Ames
11. Frank Surridge
12. David Driscoll
13. Hilda Parish
14. Robert Daniels
15. Eric Thurston
16. Rosie Grant
17. David Peneger
18. David Sims
19. Rosemary Griggs
20. Robert Daniels
    (I couldn't resist putting this one in)